MW01592972

Check MATE

A Woman's Place:
The Ultimate Challenge

TERRI JACKSON-TYLER PH.D.

AuthorHouse™
1663 Liberty Drive, Suite 200
Bloomington, IN 47403
www.authorhouse.com
Phone: 1-800-839-8640

Requests for information should be addressed to:
Publishing Co.

First published by AuthorHouse 9/12/2008

Unless otherwise indicated, all Scripture quotations are taken from the King James
Version of the Bible. Copyright 1979, 1980, 1982, by Thomas Nelson, Inc.

Chapter Diagram drawings by Ms. Shirley Mitchell
Graphic art Cover designed by Wick's Design

ISBN: 978-1-4343-9102-5 (sc)
ISBN: 978-1-4343-9101-8 (hc)

Printed in the United States of America
Bloomington, Indiana

This book is printed on acid-free paper.

authorHOUSE®

Chess Objectives:

The Queen (woman) is to make defensible moves that constitute safe territory for the King (man). The Queen's movement is designed to inhibit all threats and defeat the opponent. The Queen's overall strategy is to stay positioned until it is time to defend and support the condition of the kingdom. The Queen is to utilize her power to prevent the capture of the King. The Queen's primary function is to support the King, and to avoid being placed in direct opposition to the King.

For the man is not of the woman; but the woman of the man. Neither was the man created for the woman; but the woman for the man.

"*What a remarkable book! This book describes just how powerful and unconquerable a woman should be.*"

Elder James Runnels, Sr..
Pastor
The Greater Holmes Street
Church of God in Christ

"*This book challenges the role of women in today's society and is a call for women to accept God's ultimate challenge.*"

Alice B. Johnson
First Lady
The Johnson Christian Center

"*A painter's brush is his instrument of expression, and this artist's pen has the beauty and clarity to challenge women from a biblical perspective.*"

Bishop C. Lendon Smith
Faith Assembly Christian Center

"*As a woman in leadership roles, I can appreciate Dr. Tyler's ten winning strategies to making the right move.*"

Katie A. Arnette, Ph.D.
EEO Director, Dallas Office, BICE
Department of Homeland Security

"*This book is the most interesting volume. It is quite different from most women's perspective of partnerships.*"

Charles A. Humphrey, Ph.D.
Professor of Sociology
Paul Quinn College

"*This is a thought-provoking, must read for women interested in learning new strategies to improve their relationships.*"

Shewanda Riley
Editor of the Dallas Weekly
Published Author of "Love Hangover"

Dedications of Honor

To my husband, Darryl D. Tyler, who has been my motivator and sole inspiration to overcome and triumph in all areas of my life. I would like to express my appreciation and gratitude to you for always proving your love to me.

To my mother, Mary L. Payne, who has demonstrated unconditional love to me. I would like to thank you for being the example of a Godly mother.

To my sons, Steven and Cedric Dunn, who has been the center of my joy, Thank you both for being a constant reminder of my reason for living.

And to my best friend, Yolanda Turner, who has shared thirty-one (31) years of great memories, thank you for being a lifetime friend.

To my late grandmother, Clarissa Jackson, who introduced me to the way of Holiness. I thank her for realizing my potential, and convincing me that my greatness existed within Holiness.

To my pastor, Elder James Runnels, who has preached that, now, faith is the substance of things hoped for and the evidence of things not seen. Thank you for demonstrating your faith, which has impacted my life as the evidence.

Special Acknowledgments

Special Acknowledgments to Shewanda Riley and Genie Porter for their editorial expertise. Shewanda, thank you for holding my hand through the editing and publishing portion of my journey.

Special thanks to Tuesday Hambric and Lisa Harris for taking me under their wings and teaching me the basics principles to becoming a confident inspiring writer.

I want to acknowledge DeDe Toney who, during my infancy stage, offered valuable knowledge and insight that fueled my efforts.

Many thanks to my close friends and focus group: Jeanette Eldridge, Vivian Duren, Gretchen McGaughey, Hollie Smith, Sonya Coleman, Stormie Demerson, Ninah Robinson, Jocelyn Davis, Kellye Warren, Jael Collins, Paula Miller, LaChelle Anderson, Kathy Glynn, Shantae Haymar, LaChelle Brooks, Cassandra Cooper, and Grace Villard, for keeping me focused on what is important in life, good friends.

To my prayer partner, Virginia Caldwell, who for many years has interceded for me and shared unwavering faith. You have been a strong tower of power, thanks for being a treasured jewel.

Also, I want to acknowledge Valerie Thomas for being the definition of a friend; loyal, supportive, honest and accepting of God's plan for my life from the very beginning. Thank you for supporting my every endeavor with genuineness.

Table of Contents

Forward

The challenge has been extended. Therefore we ought to give the more earnest heed to the things which we have heard, lest at any time we should let them slip. [Hebrews 2:1]

Terri D. Jackson-Tyler has done a plausible job in discovering a woman's place in the home, church and in our society. We must not fall short or drift away, but we must be certain our anchor holds and grips the solid rock which is Jesus Christ. This book is one of the most invigorating books about women that have been printed today, especially the apprehension of a woman finding and staying in her place. So, as you read this book, look at it and see the excellence of a woman. I do concur that we have a place in the church, home and the world, and Terri let us all know that our place is found in a place of strength. She gives ten winning strategies that will place each of us in a position to make the right move, and with this concept she is destined to become a winner. So I salute Terri and encourage her to continue to write more logical and fascinating books for women. God has called for the cunning woman like Terri to reach a generation for a time such as this.

District Missionary
Mother Sweetie A. Jordan-Lacy

Preface

How many women realize that a woman's place is by divine design? Through many comparative studies, much research and from personal experience, I have found that the woman was created to improve, empower and enhance the man. She was created to multiply and add, not to subtract or divide. The woman was designed to bring an ambiance of wholesomeness by her mere presence. A woman's place is noticeably different from the man's because of the female dynamic, behavior and emotion.

Together, these attributes create very distinctive differences from the man, but in the kingdom of God man and woman are equal. The difference does not limit or prohibit a woman's ability to excel in any capacity towards growth. In modesty and subjection, this rule sets her apart and in a delicate position which is placed in wisdom. It is in this place that she discovers her power. It is vital that a woman acknowledge a man's place and willingly respect his position of responsibility.

A woman's position and the importance of her power reminds me of chess, the greatest skilled game ever invented known as the oldest war game. Chess means "King." The King is the unquestioned authority; he is the most distinguished piece on the board. Squares on the chessboard represent many cross sections in life we are oftentimes positioned to make moves based on rules; thus the analogy of the game of chess as relates to the game of life. Once the players have incorporated the rules, everything that is learned will be used as a strategy to judge, analyze and observe the moves of their opponent.

Albeit, the pieces on the chessboard are not designed to move in the same direction, they do move toward achieving the same goal. One wrong move can determine if the King's opponent is in a better position to win the battle.

Imagine life as a chess game and our world as a giant chessboard. We all are players in the game, trying to consider the right move that will ultimately result in life's triumphs or defeats. The major players are the King, which represents the man, and the Queen which represents the woman, and then there is the Bishop which represents the church. The other players are the King's soldiers. The Bishop and the Castle are a strong combination that work together to establish a safe kingdom for the King and Queen. All players must defend the King because his surrender means the loss of the kingdom. The woman, who represents the Queen, is the power behind the throne, and she can move any distance to protect the King.

Although the Queen is challenged to defend the King, she must develop a retreat plan to also protect herself from the opponent. The Queen has many places she can move to defend and protect her Castle, but she is strategically positioned next to the King to effectively demonstrate her power. The ultimate lesson in the game of chess is not how to win, but knowing what strategies to use to win. A woman should be in a place to preserve and shield the family structure from outside attacks.

It is my intention to bring awareness of the divine design to women by asking the question, "Where is your place, and will you sacrificially contribute your uniqueness to the man to support and defend his position?" Some admit that a woman's place is beside the man because God took the rib from Adam's side to create the woman. Reluctantly, some will admit that a woman's place is behind the man; if she is placed behind him, she will be protected by him. Then there are those that say a woman's place is in front; this conclusion is drawn because some believe the man has given up his right to lead.

Finding your unique place as a modern woman has become increasingly difficult because the traditional place of a woman has changed, even in the church, I will embellish this issue within the chapters to come.

Do we as women really recognize our place in the church? Leadership roles in the church have also changed, and the importance of ladyhood has diminished. The feminine side of a woman is less and less noticeable. I think one reason this resulted is because of the pressures of life and the emphasis placed on women's roles outside the home, oftentimes forcing women to lead. Therefore, roles in the home, church, work and play have resulted in deception and confusion. Forced leadership has notably confused the roles of authority in churches and in the home. We will discuss the ten strategic moves that will enable a woman to find that place of grace. These moves will be the most powerful moves that a woman can make to bring unpredicted victory into her life.

More needs to be written about this controversial issue, especially capturing the true interpretation of scriptures regarding a woman's place. I feel this issue is not being dealt with because of deep doctrinal differences. This book will attempt to clarify some of those scriptural differences by identifying the many places a woman can move to enter into her prominent place of power.

The key to understanding the place of grace is to maintain your position in the presence of God, and to operate in wisdom. The heart of the matter is the woman's power; when she is positioned in wisdom, the truth will lead her to her place. Another important key that is often ignored, and sometimes just simply overlooked by those who seek excuses rather than the truth, is the woman's place has been ordained by God, therefore it is not left up to her to choose her place.

Society sends the message that a woman's place is merely left up to choice and she should decide her place as it relates to the man. As you will see in later chapters, we will explore the scriptures to find where God has placed the woman. Contrary to all logical explanations and research, there is Biblical evidence that gives an answer, and it begins in the Garden of Eden. As history gives the account, from the very beginning, Eve was out of her place. Her discussion with the serpent should not have taken place. It was Adam's place as man over all creatures to use his authority to reproof and correct the serpent, but before he could step into his divine place of order, Eve had already eaten the forbidden fruit and offered it to Adam.

One must acknowledge that because Eve went out front, mankind is forever cursed. Eve, refusing to obey and not willing to move into a place of wisdom, placed judgment upon us all. She moved into a place of proliferated sin, causing permanent damage to mankind. A woman's place is according to God's divine direction, and He has granted her the ability to move into many positions, but her power is in her place.

The church's response when asked "Is a woman's place behind the man?" is simply put, "it depends." The church's perspective has been just as misguided and misdirected with the idea of a woman's place behind the pulpit. The church has also desensitized the importance of a woman maintaining ladyhood in her place. In other words, you will find women who mount the pulpit impersonating a man in their delivery of the Word.

Personally, I agree that the goal is to "proclaim" the gospel, and the anointing will use whomever. But can a woman not maintain the attributes of a lady instead of delivering her message in the style of a man? The anointing of God is all wise, and winning souls in wisdom is more effective. I believe the answer lies within the Holy Scriptures. When it refers to "usurp authority," it clearly speaks to women in the church regarding church leadership. [I Timothy 2:12] The Bible is unmistaken concerning the freedom and liberty of a woman, but it does not put her in a place of authority, and certainly does not allow her to assume leadership responsibilities over men.

Understand the difference when I say responsibility, being responsible for one's soul and leading one to salvation are not the same. We all are capable of leading souls to Christ, but shepherding one's soul is a position of greater responsibility. God has definitely given the woman ministry power, and that power enables her to operate at a level of leadership, her power is God's wisdom.

A woman can demonstrate confidence in every area of her life, even in ministry. A woman in her position has power in her place, and God will honor her prayers and anoint her household. A woman in position has gained the place of holiness based on her obedience; she has the power of divine order and this place of strength follows her every endeavor. She becomes honored, highly favored, and God hears her heart and will bless her home.

Many women have not found their place and will reluctantly accept the answer to their ordained position. When we are not sure of our place, we are not sure of God's plan for our lives. Here is a hint; Adam was first formed, then Eve. [1 Timothy 2:13] The verse continues to state that Adam was not deceived, but the woman being deceived was in transgression. Submission in the Old Testament was viewed as the veil of purity. Women wore veils as a sign of their love, devotion, subjection and fidelity to their husbands. It was a sign of respect and humility. Paul of the New Testament also talks about the order of creation in [1 Corinthians 11:8-12.] This order, according to God's word in verse eleven explains that both man and woman have their place, function, *purpose, calling and responsibility according to his or her relationship with Christ. "Nevertheless neither is the man without the woman, neither the woman without the man."*

When Paul discusses the "head" in the earlier verses, he is referring to the function of authority. This deals with the church's customs and worshipping styles of that day. We can relate to this concept because of the principles of partnership, and every partnership must have a head. In today's society, we should place ourselves under the same order of authority. To acknowledge God's order of creation and respect, honor and support the head. God has ordained that man be the head of the partnership, even though neither man nor woman is independent of the other.

This book is intended to clarify that there is a major difference between a helpmeet (helpmate) and checkmate. A helpmate is a person who contributes to the fulfillment of another person's need; one who is an invaluable assistant, aid, a priceless helper. Out of Adam, a helpmeet was formed by God. The Hebrew word "keneghdo" means helpmeet or suitable mate. It also means to be supportive, to be like-minded, and to be a counterpart. The woman was created as a suitable helper for man mentally, physically and morally.

The female was created in the image of man's likeness, she was created as the ultimate source of affection to man. Adam was not deceived by the serpent, but persuaded by his wife, Eve. In the game of chess, this move is considered a checkmate; this is a place where the opponent can conquer and destroy. It is said that when trust is violated, or compromise is made, then innocence vanishes. After we have sinned disobedience takes place, then we become overshadowed with fear, regret, brokenness, and shame. The awareness of truth appears transparent, and it is at that moment the knowledge of the truth of good and evil is revealed, and enmity begins.

Here lies the reason for the challenge: Eve stepped out of her place in front of the man and chose wrong over right, and then she led Adam into a place of sorrow and defeat. It is of paramount importance for us not to trivialize this historic event, but to bring this injurious cycle to an end.

*In conclusion, we must establish a relentless pursuit to triumph in a place of submission. Being in position is being purposed and prepared, becoming that suitable helpmate; becoming willing to make the right move and allow the man to make a kingly stand. Renaissance ladies, we are not placed next to the man to be the first to attack him, yet we are placed as needed to be chess masters to defend him before the enemy strikes with his final move, called "**CheckMate**."*

Dr. Terri Jackson - Tyler

Compromise: a polite type of love

Strategy 1

The Art of the Game

A chess set is a collection of game pieces. Each side gets an assortment of sixteen different pieces. Each position will be illustrated at the start of every the game.

"Square one"

Strategy 1

The Art of the Game

Genesis 3:6

When the woman saw that the fruit of the tree was good for food and pleasing to the eye, and also desirable for gaining wisdom, she took some and ate it. She also gave some to her husband, who was with her, and he ate it.

*C*onsider what I say and the Lord will give thee understanding in all things. The game of chess makes one of the most important contributions to the process of life. Inherent in it are the basic principles of specific learning theory: Strategy, Trust Recognition, Decision-making, and Self-reinforcement. All of these variables interact during the game of chess and produce the results of the strategic thought process: a win or a loss. In order to understand the game of chess, it is vital to reflect upon the beginning and learn the history and position of every player.

In a Chess game, each player has one of two sets of pieces that are distinguished by two different colors. The game is played with 32 pieces *(16 for each player)* on an eight by eight board. *(see page 1)* Each set has sixteen pieces, each with its own pattern of movement: The Rooks begin in the corners, the Knights next to the Rooks, the Bishops next to the Knights, and then the King and the Queen. Unlike the other pieces, the Pawns which are placed on the front rows can move in only one direction-forward. Once it reaches the final rank, the Pawn can transform itself into any other piece, though almost always into a Queen. The game continues with both sides taking turns until checkmate occurs, or one player resigns or both players agree to a draw. In the game of life the same holds true that each player must learn to observe his or her own strategy and recognize the important aspects of their position. In short, the player is conditioned to compete with his ultimate goal being that of attainment.

The art of the game is a woman understanding that when she is subordinate to her husband, it is merely a reflection of her subordination to Christ. She needs to recognize that possessing a skilled mind to operate in wisdom is the art of the game, only then can she realize the importance of her strategic purpose. Life is a game, a battle of forces between good and evil. A woman must not surrender to her intuitions or emotions, but she must be equipped with an inner strength of discernment, which is also the art of the game.

There are two differing schools of thought in regards to subordination and how it relates to a woman's place. The first school of thought is that the woman was created equal in all respects to man and can be placed in roles of authority, headship and leadership over men. The other thought is, although the woman is whole and was created equal to man; she was specifically created as man's second half, as partner, as helpmeet (helpmate).

God planned the creation of woman in great detail to show that the woman and man relate to each other with roles of distinction. God said in [Genesis 2:18, 23] "It is not good that man should be alone; I will make a help meet for him." It is clear here that God's primary reason for creating woman was first and foremost for man. Many commentaries state that man was only half of God's plan for human life, and the woman was the other half. God's plan was incomplete and imperfect without woman. The other school of thought is found in Matthew Henry's commentary, it states that the woman was taken from Adam's side; not from his head to rule over him, not from his feet to be trampled on, but from under his arm to protect, taken from close to his heart to be loved. The woman's place of companionship becomes a place of divine duty.

What is clear about both of these schools of thought is that they agree and believe that the woman has a special role. Because of so many beliefs, we see major differences of opinion concerning a woman's role and limitations.

From a Biblical perspective, one point of controversy is centered on the question of "what is the true interpretation of the scripture [I Corinthians 11:3] "and what is meant by "the head of the woman is man." [Ephesians 5:22-25] Following the hierarchy structure of creation and God's chain of command, He created Adam, then came Eve [1 Timothy 2:11-13]. The Apostle Paul states that, the head of the woman is the man and the head of Christ is God. One is not better than the other, but for order and accountability purposes, the woman was ordained by God to be subordinate to the man. God gave explicit instructions to the first couple of the human race, to Adam then to Eve, but because of their sin, then came the fall of humanity through disobedience.

Now we understand why Eve was deceived, but Adam, he acted willfully and was deliberate in his rebellion against God. Observe how Adam and Eve's God-given positions changed because of sin. Adam's position of being the head of mankind suddenly changed to being the helpmate to Eve. Eve became the head, making important decisions for mankind. Their positions were interchanged; thus, the problem of placement role reversal began.

Because Eve was out of place she was completely won over by Satan's cunning conversation, not realizing that she would not be ready to accept responsibility for her actions. Eve was unaware of the full extent of her disobedience. Although Adam understood he was about to sin, he was determined not to survive Eve, so he ate of the fruit because of his love for Eve. One can only guess that Adam adhered to Eve offering him the fruit to avoid being separated from her. Adam being overwhelmed continued to eat of the fruit realizing the weight of his sin, but immediately blamed Eve, then Eve blamed the serpent, the serpent blamed God. Neither Adam, Eve nor the serpent were willing to fully accept what they had done, but God was about to hand down to each of them their punishment according to their acts of disobedience. Satan had three personal strategies that he used to plant the seeds of doubt into Eve's mind, she yielded to what she felt, saw and desired. [1 John 2:16] They both fell into the place of temptation

"A threefold damnation":

1. *Lust of the flesh* = *good for food* = *pleasure*
2. *Lust of the eyes* = *pleasant to the eyes* = *possession*
3. *Pride of life* = *desirable to make one wise* = *power*

This verse explains how Adam and Eve got caught up in their world. Verses 15 and 16 tell us not to love the world nor the things in the world. If anyone loves the world, the love of the Father is not in him. Adam and Eve were in love with the things around them and not in love with the things of God.

In the fourth chapter of the book of Matthew, Satan tempted Jesus with things of the world, in the areas of pleasure, possession and power. These are areas of human desire that we struggle with because, in like manner, we will be tempted. Dr. David Jeremiah, radio pastor of "Turning Point Ministry" in El Cajon, California, states that we have the normal desires of human nature which are to desire pleasure, possession and power. They are God given desires, but Satan has distorted these desires from God's human nature to his sinful nature.

The outcome in which God dealt with Adam and Eve and the consequences of his judgment against disobedience were devastating. It gives insight on how we should consider God's wisdom in many of our present day dilemmas. In verse 16 of chapter 3 in the book of Genesis you will find the reason that women face the rebellion of submitting to men, and an explanation of why men have the authority to rule. The curse given upon the woman was that she would lose her position as man's equal and become subject to him.

After Adam and Eve sinned then came the consequences; one of the curses for the woman was that she would be condemned to a state of sorrow and subjection. The woman was placed in a state of temptation and subjection; she was created equal to man in the beginning, but because of the fall she is placed in a supportive role. She is not inferior to the creation of man, but is subject to his position of responsibility. This is the same hierarchy of male leadership that Paul spoke of when explaining the woman's role in the home [Colossians 3:18-19] and [1 Peter 3:1-7], which are clear commandments that are extended to the man. He is a "servant-leader." The curses noted in [Genesis 3:16] are God's commandments not his comments. "He (the husband) shall rule over thee (the wife)." This statement means the woman was placed under the condition of humble subjection to the man. When God set this judgment, it was not meant to condemn the position of the woman. God was setting the family in order, establishing structure. The family needed a head, someone to rule the family. It was set in order by God for the man to be the head, not the woman. This judgment applies to each man individually; it does **not** mean all men are over all women. It means that every wife is subject to her own husband, not subject to all men, or a mere companion.

The sentencing that God placed on Adam and Eve as punishment carries throughout the existence of eternity until the New Jerusalem is established. Therefore, throughout the Old and New Testament this commandment applies to the woman and is still valid and operative. The struggle for women will continue if we don't accept the judgment of rulership. To understand this struggle and to accept what has been ordained, women will move into a place of grace that will bring a greater importance to their planned purpose. The scripture states that God formed Eve, which means He put her in a place; a place of protection, a place of strength. This is why verses in Ephesians and Colossian relate directly to the explanation of a woman's place; "Wives, submit to your husbands as to the Lord." [Ephesians 5:22] If the woman had not sinned, she would always have obeyed with humility and meekness. If man had not sinned, he would always have ruled with wisdom and love. Because Eve gave up her place to Satan and lost all reason and judgment, because of this the woman is not called to a place of authority over men. She does on the other hand have her place of order in society, the church, politics and the home.

Titus gives some good examples of the basic roles of a woman's place in the home. [*Titus 2: 3-5*], Titus suggests to the aged women that their behavior become holy, and that they should admonish the young women to love their husbands and their children. Titus also advised to the aged women to teach the younger women to be discreet, chaste, keepers at home, discerned, and to be obedient. Realize and understand that "place" is not a state of being, or a level of degradation. It is a role of duty, a state of surrender. Life's struggles have forced many women to be strong women and at times being strong can mean losing sight of being a woman of strength. The solution to becoming a woman of strength is to reveal that your weakness is your strength. Meaning that your weakness is unto obedience, and to become that weaker vessel is to demonstrate the strength of Christ.

Because of the changes in our culture and the change of times, a change has occurred in our concept of virtue. Women in the Bible were ladies regardless of their aggressive or passive personality; they were respectful, devoted and obedient as they feared God. God created temperaments of uniqueness; these women were beautiful from the inside out, they exemplified their beauty from the outside by demonstrating God's power from within.

Prayer

Father, in the name of Jesus,
I am so grateful that You designed me to be unique and graceful.
My worth is far more valuable than jewels.
Father, I am so grateful that Your Word leads me to my place. I
accept and receive that my position is to serve and worship You.
I acknowledge that I was created to be a suitable mate.
I walk in the spirit of wisdom demonstrating Godliness in my
conduct, character, and conversation daily.
I praise Your name for being the God of wisdom that I seek.
In the matchless name of Jesus,
Amen.

Sacrifice: A precious offering

Strategy 2

before castling   after castling

The Art of Sacrifice

There is one special type of move made by a King and a Rook simultaneously. It is called castling.

Strategy 2

The Art of Sacrifice

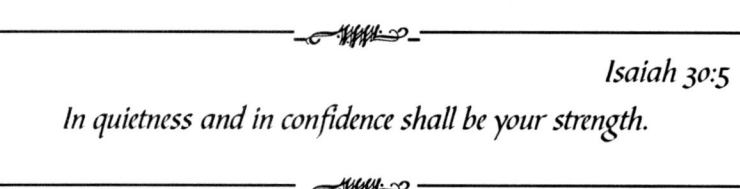

Isaiah 30:5
In quietness and in confidence shall be your strength.

There are special conditions when we must make special moves. This is true both in the game of life and in a chess game. One of these special moves is called castling. It is where players move two pieces simultaneously. Generally, a King and Rook make this move under certain conditions. *(See diagram 2 on page 13)* Although this move is placing the Rook in a risky position, it also has the advantages of putting the King where he is less likely to be attacked. The Queen, on the other hand, cannot castle; she must never be placed in a position that places her King in a vulnerable position. Within a relationship, this move by a woman is usually mistaken as weakness. She should never put the man in a place of attack. "But what if he deserves it?" Many women will justify being provoked to doing so, but the best strategy in this condition is to use wisdom.

This calls for a special move, it is moving into a place of surrender. A woman who surrenders is a woman who takes an active position of sacrifice to think of the spiritual outcome before she makes any moves. In the book "Words to live by for women," published by Bethany House, the unknown author defines the word sacrifice as: to surrender something of intrinsic value in order to accomplish a spiritual good. To sacrifice is to surrender, to surrender is to compromise. Compromise can also be translated as "love" and for a woman to sacrifice is also a challenge in demonstrating her reverence to the man. To be in a state of surrender is the ultimate sacrifice and spiritual victory.

Paul, the writer of Ephesians, encourages the man to love his wife as Christ also loved the church, as he gave himself for it; he also instructs the wife to reverence her husband. Paul makes it clear that the love which the husband is to have for his wife is a deeper love, a spiritual love. Just as Christ's love for the church is a sacrificial love, the art of sacrifice, is supreme love. A woman's victory is in the place of supreme sacrifice; both the man and woman can achieve personal triumph when the act of sacrifice is practiced. A man should have power to love a woman into having the right attitude. In turn, the woman should have the right attitude to have the power to love the man. Having this knowledge is demonstrated by the power of example. It is easy to fall in love with the idea of being in love, but having a sacrificial love determines if it is true love. Dr. J. Vernon McGee, of the "Thru the Bible" radio broadcast in Pasadena, California, said in his notes and outlines that "even Rahab the harlot represented faith. She placed herself as a sacrifice for the men of God. This exemplifies that one's sacrifice can be a supreme act of faith." In scripture Peter commands: "the man to dwell with the woman according to knowledge, giving honor unto the wife, as unto the weaker vessel, and as being heirs together of grace of life."

A woman's knowledge may sometimes be compromised. At this point, she realizes she has power and can clearly discern that she can make a difference. According to God's instructions regarding a woman, her level of conviction and obedience will establish her place. It is also in Godly confidence that she understands that in quietness she masters her strength. Her strength is being sound in speech and knowing when to speak is definitely one very critical attribute to include in mastering the art of sacrifice.

As it is in the game of chess, any move can compromise your position, especially the position of the King. One bad move and it could dismantle his kingdom. Oftentimes, to sacrifice is to relinquish something at the cost of your logic, this may, at times, leave you appearing obtuse. All the players' positions in a chess game can be sacrificed for the King. The Queen, at times, will have to forfeit her position in order to protect her King.

The deception in our society is that a woman's sacrifice is viewed as loss of right and loss of expression. When a man is walking in his divine authority, there are times when a woman will become powerless. It is all according to God's divine gameplan for the woman to walk in order and structure with the man in propriety. In actuality, the Queen takes inclusive control, and if her power is appreciated and accepted in divine order, the King will get the opportunity to rule during every battle against his opponent. Ruling is the nature of a much deserved victory. This is a case where the kingdom will not be forced to self-destruct. The idea of a man ruling and having authority over a woman is put into perspective. It can only benefit and protect the woman at the cost of her sacrifice. The King in the game of chess is considered the head, but the Queen has the power to destroy the kingdom at her discretion.

In the 14th chapter of Proverbs, Solomon wrote, "every wise woman buildeth her house; but the foolish plucketh it down with her hands." *[Proverbs 14:1]* It is important to understand how this works; the man is the authority in the home and church, which justifies his grounds as an accepted source of expert knowledge and the power to command. The woman is that power behind this justified authority. Power is defined as having the absolute ability to do something with strength, force and might. This means that the Queen has the authority to be powerful, but to use graceful power and to operate in wisdom.

The Queen operates in wisdom by first identifying her position in all states of affairs; then she focuses on the purpose, plans her actions, and focuses on her best qualities which are patience and quietness. In this, she determines positive outcomes. This graceful power is demonstrated through divine effectiveness, and this type of power allows a woman to understand her place and operate accordingly. A woman can use her power in a state of authority and not be considered "the authority." This means the woman is subject to the man in the sense that she acknowledges that he is the commanded head, but she is that power that shields, enhances his position.

It is apparent when an unwise woman operates out of control instead of in the power of wisdom. She will plant a seed of doubt and become distracted like Eve in the garden, unaware of Satan's tactics of deception. The sacrifice of the game is the spirit of obedience. What happens more often in an actual game of chess is that a player will imagine an advantageous board position, and then will work toward making that position a reality. This approach almost always wins the game, with much pain comes much reward, and strength will come in quietness and confidence. *[Isaiah 30:15]* In this game, the King has the opportunity to attack and rule his opponent's kingdom. The pursuit to conquer the opponent's kingdom is to rule with absolute victory. The King is appointed to rule in his kingdom; therefore, if the King is being weakened by a challenge, it means his defense has been weakened within his own castle.

It is important that the research of Biblical word and meanings are understood and that we rid ourselves of misleading and inaccurate translations. Take, for instance, the word "rule." The root word for "rule" in Hebrew is "mashal" which means, to govern, to lead, to command. The correct meaning is especially important in order to capture true meaning, this continues to apply in the new covenant. The King has rights to exercise authority within the constraints of his kingdom as a man, within God's structure and standards of his home. He is also warranted to live under a rule of ultimate law and order; he himself is governed by a higher authority. Many times the concept of "rule" can be distorted by the over zealous attitude to express control that leads to misappropriated power, which, is seldom found in equally yoked relationships. The man will deem to abuse his authority by unreasonable demands and commands, regardless of his inappropriate, unkingly behavior. His position is usually to be acknowledged as one which is the authority in all things, but accepts responsibility only in some things. This is not a true demonstration of a King ruling his kingdom; this is a King of dishonor, ruling without noble cause.

A wise woman operates as fitting unto the Lord, and her submission is rendered under the watchful eye of Christ equating the husband's position as it relates to Christ and the Church

Prayer

Father, I come to you in the name of Jesus. Thanking You for providing me with mercy and grace. I reverence and worship Your name.

Thank You for the spirit of quietness, for this is where I find my strength.
Help me, dear Lord to surrender my will to Your word.
Lord, I know that my victory is in the place of superior sacrifice to You.
I praise You for being a God of sacrifice and divine order.
In the matchless name of Jesus,
Amen.

Submit: A voluntary surrender

Strategy 3

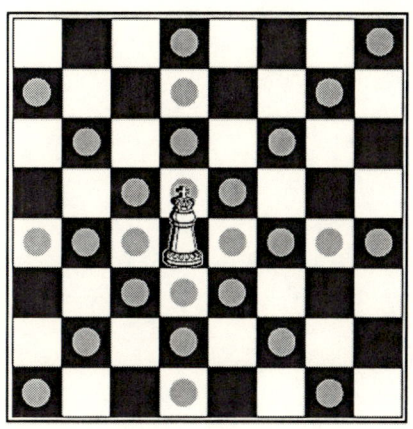

The Art of Defense

---

*To facilitate notation of moves, all squares are given names,
consisting of the combination of its letter-column and number-row.*

Strategy 3

The Art of Defense

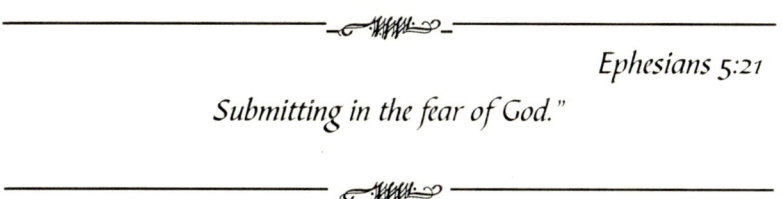

Ephesians 5:21

Submitting in the fear of God."

hess is played on a checkered board with 64 dark and light squares. The white and black Queens both begin the game on squares of their color. All squares are identified by letters and numbers in order to record and make chess notations. *(See diagram 3 on page* 23) The game begins with white making the first move.

In a chess game, tactics refers to traps and tricks or combinations that achieve checkmate advantages within a few moves; strategy refers to achieving long-term goals through the proper arrangement of the pieces on the board in the absence of any short-term opportunities. In life, however, biblical strategy is just the opposite of the world's strategies and rules. Players must develop principles of biblical rule that will obtain immediate knowledge to achieve the promise of life's end game result, which spiritually is eternal life.

The book of Genesis explains that God made the woman unique. A woman's defense is not to be in opposition to the man, but to be placed where she can express her uniqueness. She was fashioned with a tender and sensitive nature; God placed upon her his finishing touch as He completed the creation of mankind. There are many misrepresentations of the word "submission." One major misconception of the meaning is "to give up all power," or to have limited control. The word "submit" in the Greek is "hypotasso" which means to "distinguish" to identify with the man and to discover that his position is an ordained chain-of-command, God's structure of authority. The truth of the matter is, to give less is to give more when one submits. The position of submission is humility. Jesus Christ, the Son of God, who being in the form of God, did not consider himself equal with God, but took upon himself the form of a servant, and was made in the likeness of men; and being found in fashion as a man, he humbled himself, and became obedient unto death, even the death of the cross. [Philippians 2:5-8] A woman who submits is actually gaining more power and more control through her willingness to submit. The woman's weapon is wisdom, and her best defense is knowing when to utilize her power and control. This is skillfully mastered by walking in the spirit of wisdom. This defense also empowers her to become reserved in her actions, words and deeds. She is then able to enter into a place of victory in every area of her life. This is considered the Godly-achieved woman. On the contrary, you will discover that there are other types of women who relate to power and control differently than the Godly achieved woman:

1. **Over-achieving Woman** - *she is afraid to lose control - this woman has a desire only to lead and she is not willing to follow.*

*2. **Under-achieving Woman** - she is out of control - this woman does not want to lead, nor does she wants to follow.*

*3. **Achieved Woman** - she is in control - this woman is only willing to follow when it is convenient for her to follow.*

*4. **Godly Achieved Woman** - she is controlled by the Holy Spirit – this woman is willing to follow.*

Three of these positions conflict with the Godly achieved woman; a woman who establishes her control based on the spiritual submission of obedience. *[Proverbs 24:3]* states: "By wisdom a house is built, and through understanding it is established."

A wise woman operates as fitting unto the Lord, and her submission is rendered under the watchful eye of Christ, equating the husband's position as it relates to Christ and the Church. *[Colossians 3:18]* The principle of submission is not from a natural perspective. The grounds for submission are expressions of respect and reverence for headship. As women, our duty is to love unto obedience, and the husband's duty is to give us tender love and care. Each relationship has a measure of duty as to the obedience of Christ unto the cross. A woman is obedient to the man's position of responsibility, not to his actual power. Submission is a place of surrender, surrender is place of duty, and duty is a state of mind, not a state of being; submission is a state of meekness- not a state of weakness. Job explains that if we submit to God and are at peace with him, prosperity will follow. *[Job 22:21]*

Submission has to be placed in perspective. Submission is altogether different for a single woman; it is not biblical that a single woman must submit to the opposite sex. *[1 Corinthians 7:34]* states, "There is a difference between a wife and a virgin, the unmarried woman cares about the things of the Lord, that she may be holy both in body and in spirit." A single woman must exhaust her energies towards the things of God. She must commit to submit her will to God's will. To be single in Christ is to be satisfied with presenting yourself holy and sanctified for the use of the kingdom. *1 Peter 4: 15 states*, "But let none of you suffer as a Christian, let him not be ashamed, but let him glorify God in this manner." The scriptures clearly relate to wives submitting to their own husbands. It is oftentimes difficult for a married woman to use practical ways to be submissive as she finds herself challenged to submit when her husband is not demonstrating his position of responsibility.

An example of how submission can easily be misunderstood is when the single man in the relationship is demanding that his companion who is single should be obedient to him, and submit to his request. As he continues to disrespect and ignore her plea for affection, she finds it difficult to submit or compromise with him. Whether single or married in this situation the woman must first see this matter through spiritual eyes and be very prayerful to not make the wrong move. This is a situation that warrants the spirit of wisdom, and it is a matter that needs urgent attention, yet requires patience to accomplish lasting results. Submission for a single woman is unto God, once married it becomes a vow unto the husband.

[*I Peter 3:9*] says "not returning evil for evil or reviling for reviling, but on the contrary blessing, knowing that you were called to this, that you may inherit a blessing. Submission is mutual; it is yielding unto one another according to the scriptures. To submit is to have a Godly desire to become a servant and having the discipleship of dedication to submit yourselves one to another. Submission is best understood as "yieldedness," to voluntarily surrender your will to another. Yielding is serving; to serve one is to offer service. As a waiter serves in a restaurant, he or she is giving of themselves with no expectation they are performing a desired duty, and this is servanthood. There is a difference between servitude and servanthood, but our society has made them indistinguishable. Mr. Probst, who only wanted to be described as a devoted man of God, expressed in conversation a profound observation regarding the misconception of these two words. He stated, "We find ourselves using the words submission and servitude synonymously, and over the years they have migrated to become one word with the same definition. When in reality the word and their terms have extremely different meanings."

For instance, servitude is a state of subjection to another person; the condition of being bound to service. It is the condition of being in bondage. Servitude is a state of subjection where one becomes master and forces labor upon another. It is when one becomes subject to another's command - servitude is weakness. A servant is a person who willfully, he serves others voluntarily. Serving has real meaning only when a person performs labor or exerts himself for the benefit of another without expectations servanthood is meekness. When we as women submit unto any authority, it is in the fear of God that we surrender unto the servanthood of Christ; we owe Him, no one else.

Our grounds of submission are inferior to the degree of servanthood as it relates to Christ. Being submissive is being a servant; it is not rendering servitude or having a lack of personal freedom. To be submitted is to consider the sacrifice of a servant, and surrender the cost of any compensation. The formula below will help you distinguish between a spirit of servanthood or servitude. The formula is:

1. Servitude =To serve, to wait as labor

          Condition of labor + expectation of compensation

          (any kind) = servitude

2. Servanthood = to surrender compromise

          Submission of love + volunteer service = servanthood

Our mission, method and message are sacrifices,
but the act of sacrifice is not at the cost of being miserable.
That's not God's ministry"

Prayer

*F*ather, I come to You in the name of Jesus. I come before Your
presence with a submitted heart. I lift myself up to You totally
willing
to understand my place of submission.
I walk in submission to You. I totally surrender to the obedience
of Your Word and Your ways.
I resist everything that will exalt itself above Your Word.
I cast down all vain imaginations that will lead me to a place of
deception.
I declare that my life is filled with Your loving kindness.
Teach me, Oh lord, to submit to the leadership of the Holy Spirit.
I praise you for being a God of provision.
In the matchless name of Jesus,
Amen.

Servant: Devotion to duty

Strategy 4

Using Practical Techniques

Steps one, two and three are very basic chess rules, but when explaining what happens in special conditions, there are other chess rules and steps.

Strategy 4

Using Practical Techniques

Titus 2:5

To be self-controlled and pure, to be busy at home, to be kind, and to be subject to their husbands, so that no one will malign the word of God.

The rules of Chess are easy, but the game itself can become complicated and challenging. *(See diagram 4 on page 33)* Chess is a game played by two players, each player plays with a specified goal in mind, which is to triumph over his opponent. Each player has so many players in the beginning of the game; the objective is for the winner to remain standing. As in any game, there are certain techniques and rules that are required to determine the winner. Just as for the game called life, there are techniques, as well as spiritual rules that should be used for each player. The following practical steps are developed to be mastered in every aspect of life.

The first practical technique is to set out to accomplish the *mission* of developing your identity; also spiritually you should develop who you are in Christ. The second practical step in a chess game is to develop a *method* where you control the center of the board, but from a spiritual sense your center is controlled by Christ. Lastly, the *message*, this is the sacrifice that is given; it is to protect your interest. The act of sacrifice is not at the cost of being miserable; this was not God's ministry. God was very practical in His approach and he always practiced being compassionate. Below are the three practical techniques that can help the woman to move into a higher level of wisdom;

1. *The Mission – develop your relationship with Christ*
2. *The Method – center your life around biblical principles*
3. *The Message – protect the head of the family*

God has made it clear that we are on a mission in this life. The mission is to love and seek compassion. When we are faced with challenges, we must respond with patience and obedience. The method to use is always prayer, and the message, this will be the example of your life, your personal ministry.

Our mission, method and message should clearly become representatives of our creator, so we will be light that lost souls see in darkness. These three practical steps should not only be displayed when playing the game of chess, but also displayed when exhibiting Godly character in the game of life. By giving a Godly message, with a Godly method on a Godly mission, you will capture a Godly reward. [Genesis 16:2], Sarah, Abraham's wife, displayed the attitude of uncertainty, she felt she had to manipulate the circumstances to make things happen; she laughed at the promise of God. Sarah was doubtful and impatient at the possibility of having a child at age ninety. She thought it was impossible, but through God, this unbelievable situation was possible. One faithful saying of the Bible is, not to lean on your own understanding. [Proverb 3:5] It's evident that Sarah didn't trust the Lord at first. She trusted what she could see, she came close to missing the move of God. What Sarah needed was to stop and listen with her inner ear to hear the voice of God.

Mary Magdalene's mission was accomplished because she heard and obeyed Jesus immediately. Mary's priorities were placed in order and she took the time to listen to His voice. The method of the message has meaning, and the method is simply prayer, a time to fellowship with the father, a time of dedication and worship. "Therefore I say unto you, what things soever ye desire, when ye pray, believe that ye receive them, and ye shall have them." [Mark 11:24] Prayer is spending time in quietness, finding a place in peace. Our heart and minds have to be prepared and positioned to meditate in the spirit; sincere prayer will set you up for change.

Change ushers one into the presence of answers, and it is there that you will find God, who will open the door to your heart; the power of God will uncover answers to your prayers and you will produce fruit. There is more to prayer than just uttering words; we have to understand when we pray that the answer to the prayer is according to God's will. Remember what we may consider good may not be the good of God. "Every good and perfect gift is from above." [James 1:17] "Do not take the desire of your heart for granted. But in all matters by prayer and supplication with thanksgiving let your request be made known to God." [Philippians 4:6]

Lastly, the message can also be your ministry; your misery can turn into your ministry. The misery of your fears, worries, depression, addiction, anger, hostility, deception, heartbreak, financial struggle, test of trial, and disappointment in life now, can become a message of ministry to someone later. Your deliverance is the opportunity to share your message with others. What you suffer now becomes a testimony to give later. It will be a message of deliverance, triumph and victory. You can share this message with someone who is in need of a millennium witness. Your rocky marriage may become your ministry. Your drinking problem may become a ministry. That bad situation on the job may become your ministry. The effects of that failed long-term relationship can be used as a ministry. That business proposal that was turned down, it is your ministry. Sharing the message of deliverance to someone is God's way of teaching us that in our weakness we are truly made strong.

Sister Eve, don't be deceived

Prayer

*F*ather, in the name of Jesus,
I am so grateful that I will not be ignorant concerning Your Word.
In Your Word, You said You would perfect that which concerns
me.
Teach me to find my mission in life. Show me the method of Your
principles.
Help me to acknowledge Your message of protecting my home.
Thank You for being a God of righteousness.
In the matchless name of Jesus,
Amen.

Power: A vigorous strength

Strategy 5

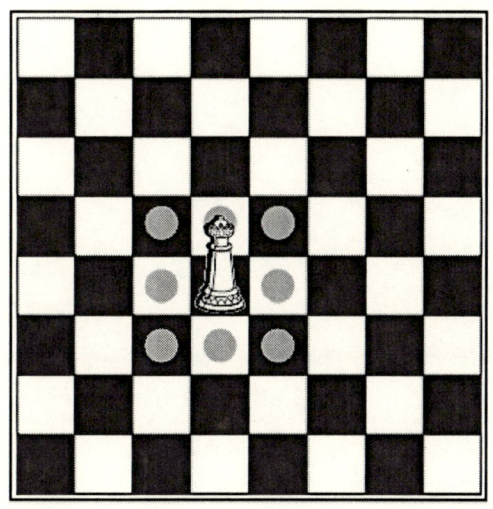

Knowing When To Move

When the King is not in check, he is mated.

Strategy 5

Knowing When To Move

---

1 Peter 3:4

Even the ornament of a meek and quiet spirit,
which is in the sight of God of great price"

A woman can move into many places to support a man. Most times, her place simply depends on her position. This is why it is important to be discerning before making any move. In today's society, women are challenged with an overwhelming sense of responsibility to compete with men and prove their equality. The roles have been reversed and women today have placed themselves out front because many men have failed at structured authority. Understand and realize that there is a more excellent way!

First, let us understand the unique way God designed the woman; then, let us try to understand why God designed the woman. *Genesis 2: 22 & 23* says, "And the rib, which the Lord God had taken from man, made he a woman, and brought her unto the man. And Adam said this is now bone of my bone, and flesh of my flesh she shall be called Woman, because she was taken out of Man." We were created by God to be a helper suitable for the man.

Recognizing when to move, and what is the best move, is knowing where you are placed. A woman in the right position has power in her place, and she knows that God has divinely positioned her in the home, in her career and anywhere else life's journey leads her.

You are to first be aligned with the will of God according to His Word. Being in this position, you can accept the wrong move which may ultimately take you in the right direction. Your conduct, character and conversation should always be parallel to God's word. This is a good indication that God has instructed you to move in the right direction.

One of the greatest military victories in the Old Testament happens under a singing servant named Deborah; she knew when and how to move. Deborah was positioned to be used by God in a leadership role, she was highly esteemed as the judge of Israel. Deborah's leadership role as judge was successful because she was in a place of obedience. She possessed an attitude of willingness; she made herself available to God and achieved victory as she reported a word of the Lord to King Barak. The King then sought her Godly knowledge and power, which later resulted in the rescue of the Israelites from the Canaanites. This great story of battle is a perfect demonstration of a woman in position who possessed power in her place and knowing when to move resulted in victory. Had Deborah stepped out on her own credentials of being a judge and not under God's direction and timing, the march to Mount Tabor against Jabin's army would have continued the persecution in the land of Israel. *[Judges 4: 6-7]*

The focus here is not to question Deborah's role of leadership, recognize her exhibition of controlled power and to examine how she used her position to bless the King and not challenge his authority even though she had the power to do so. It was in her place of leadership that she remained a lady and did not exalt herself to becoming the ultimate authority. Barak led his army's chariots, but it is evident that Deborah led their hearts. The Queen's move in the game of chess is basically the same as a woman's movement in the game of life. She has to make alternate moves to allow the man free reign to master and command his territory. The King is the most authoritative player in the game and his moves must be made in such a way to avoid being in the path of danger. To be in a state of check is to be captured on the next move. "Checkmate," is when the King has no way to extricate himself from the situation, this is when the opposition has won the game. *(See diagram 5 on page 41)* The word "Checkmate" comes from the Persian word "shahmat" which means the King is dead. This should only be carried out by the King's opponent, certainly not by the Queen or any foot soldiers residing in his castle.

A Biblical example of spiritual checkmate is found in the book of Daniel in the first and second chapters. Basically, the battle was between Nebuchadnezzar, King of Babylon, and certain children of Israel, known as Daniel, Shadrach, Meshach, and Abednego. This was the perfect chess game, as the challenge depended on what would be the next move for Daniel. As Daniel took time to study the King and became aware that the King had him checkmated; God answered Daniel's prayer and made known unto the King the interpretations of his dream concerning his kingdom. God had a master plan for the Hebrew boys and he used Daniel as a major player to save Israel. Just as God knew the next move on the board for the Hebrew boys, he knows when to place our enemy in checkmate and will do so due to our obedience. Knowing when to move, is knowing when to ask for wisdom, knowledge and understanding. Daniel was given wisdom and knowledge and was highly sought after because of his ability.

One of the secrets to a woman finding favor with her King is to be different from him; to have abilities and qualities opposite of his. A man takes pride in the numerous ways that a woman is different from him. A few valued and priceless differences that will win a man's heart include the following: tenderness by touch, tenderness in speech and the most favorable is known to be her gentle, meek and quiet spirit. This is considered being a graceful woman, displaying that softness of a woman. In some cases, it is as simple as being a lady; this approach encourages a man to stand as commanded. Having a lady present will soften the battle. It is often said that a man does not like to see the reflection of himself in a woman. A man should find simplicity, reassurance and tolerance in the strength of a woman. A belligerent and aggressive spirit is needed only on the battlefield; a meek and humble spirit is needed in the castle. With a humble spirit, a woman should be able to express the uniqueness of her divine design; this is what makes her different, but very powerful. Knowing when to follow, is knowing that the right move has been made.

Having a willing attitude to follow is a lot like learning to dance. Ballroom dancing is as simple as following the leader. Learning to tango or rumba is fun when these dance steps are being taught by the man, following becomes fun and we are willing to learn. There is no feeling of inferiority or any feelings of threat, and there is no reason to challenge his authority at this point because we are willing and have a desire to follow. This attitude of willingness should permeate our being; and the strength that is used to oppose it should be used to compromise. One who knows when to move is the one who knows how to move!

God created the woman to be a helpmate, not to be a checkmate

---

Prayer

*F*ather, in the name of Jesus,
I am so grateful that I know when to move. Your Word teaches me
that a meek and a quiet spirit is precious in your sight.
I want to be of great value in your sight, so please continue
to help me find a more excellent way.
Help me to know when and how to move to avoid Satan's tricks,
traps and schemes.
Give me the attitude of willingness to open my heart to the truth.
I praise you for being a God of power.
In the matchless name of Jesus,
Amen.

Renaissance Lady: A woman who establishes a relentless pursuit to triumph in a place of submission.

Strategy 6

The Portrait of A Queen

The Queen has the combined moves. She can move as far as she wants, in any direction on the board in a straight, horizontal, vertical, or diagonal line.

Strategy 6

The Portrait of a Queen

Proverbs 12:4

A woman of noble character is a crown,
but a disgraceful woman is like decay in the man's bones .

---

*I*n the game of chess, there are many players with many positions, but the Queen is the most important player with the most important position. The Queen can move in any direction, any distance, with any number of places as long as her path is clear. *(See diagram 6 on page 49)* The Queen cannot jump any pieces; she can only capture by occupying her place. This is why it is so important to know the right move. The Queen is also the most powerful player; she is the power behind the throne. The Queen has the power to conquer or destroy her opponent, as well as her own army. When in combat, she operates in excellence using wise strategies to maintain victory, always bearing in mind the ultimate goal, to protect the King. The Queen is not forceful, hasty, impatient or overbearing. She uses wise tactics to pursue and conquer. The character of a Queen is defined as a high standard of a lady, poised and graceful.

Externally, the Queen reflects the brilliance of her internal qualities. In a place of yieldedness, a place of surrender, a place of providence, the Queen is able to move into her position of natural order. The Queen, who represents the woman, was intended to display the wisdom, goodness, love, and strength of God. She was also created to display God's glory and to manifest His greatness and majesty. She was indeed created in God's image, but Paul also adds that the woman is the glory of the man, *[1 Corinthians 11:7]* Adam was created directly by the hand of God. Eve was also created directly by God, but was actually taken out of Adam, so the woman owes her origin to man.

More importantly, the man was created directly for God; the woman was created directly for man. So, as the moon reflects the glory of the sun, so the man reflects the glory of God and the woman reflects the glory of man. A lady is a Queen personified; she is a woman of grace. A lady is crowned with wisdom and adorned with virtue. A lady knows her place and operates in the spirit of ladyhood. A lady exudes a spirit of gentleness and is characterized by feminine qualities. The expression of ladyhood is exhibited in word and deed.

By exemplifying graceful behavior, I have coined the word ladyhood to mean a woman who exhibits the behavior that will demonstrate her desire to please God. Webster defines the word lady, as "a well-mannered and considerate woman with high standards of proper behavior, a woman regarded as proper and virtuous." A lady should always operate in a more excellent way and demonstrate wisdom in all things. Her beauty is later evident by her radiant character and inner strength.

Throughout biblical history there were many Queens who greatly influenced the church world. As we have seen in earlier chapters, these women influenced others to turn to God, but not all of the Queens in the history of the Bible were used to turn nations back to God. Some women were in place to turn an entire nation against God. This is a spirit, the "Jezebel spirit." It haunts women and men today who are standing in positions of leadership and authority, especially in the church. Jesus confronts this same spirit in the Church at Thyatira: "And to the angel of the Church in Thyatira write:

"These things say the Son of God, who has eyes like a flame of fire, and His feet like fine brass: I know your deeds, your love and faith, your service, and perseverance, and that you are now doing more than you did at first. Nevertheless, I have this against you: You tolerate that woman Jezebel, who calls herself a prophetess. By her teaching she misleads my servants into sexual immorality and the eating of food sacrificed to idols. I will strike her children dead. Then all the churches will know that I am He who searches hearts and minds." [Revelation 2:18-21, 23]

The book, Unmasking the Jezebel Spirit by John Paul Jackson, gives insight on these scriptures. He explains in his book the details about Queen Jezebel who exudes corruption, and how she encouraged an entire nation to worship idol Gods.

Jezebel was in constant disobedience and abomination to the God of Israel. This is why it is most important for women to walk in the direct guidance of God. They should be endowed with the spirit of patience, humility, wisdom and discernment; these fruits will help avoid being taken over by destructive strongholds. To merely scratch the surface concerning demonic activity and spiritual wickedness in high places, you will find in the book Pigs In The

Parlor by Frank & Ida Hammond, many ways to be delivered from these demonic forces. These forces are determined to tear God's Kingdom down, especially through those individuals who are in leadership and in authoritative roles. This spirit of destruction is rampant and still influences the body of Christ today. The spirit of Jezebel has and will continue to cripple churches unless women walk in God's appointed authority.

Please understand men are affected by this spirit also, but historically women were commonly used, and sometimes unaware of the alluring and seductive spirit that Satan often camouflaged as ministry to oppose the sincere work of God. John Paul Jackson says that this celestial power operates through deception; these demonic forces are accompanied by the spirit of manipulation, control, lust, perversion and false teachers. So it is today, as it was in those days, that the history of Jezebel's treacherous roots is generational. The spirit of Jezebel embraces not only harlotry, adultery and witchcraft, but a very forceful spirit to kill, steal and destroy leadership authority.

What we need more of today is the spirit of Elijah, women and men who will not compromise righteousness, but challenge the worship of Baal. A Godly Queen should create countermoves to demonstrate the spirit of Elijah and make great exploits that will only edify and glorify God's kingdom, even at the cost to secure and enlarge the kingdom. A Godly Queen should be prepared and molded into the woman God wants her to be. The scriptures note that the Queen of Persia, Esther, was prepared and purposed for her position which ultimately moved her into a place of appointed authority. Before Esther was Queen there was Queen Vashti. Queen Vashti disobeyed her husband and was permanently removed from her position as Queen. Queen Vashti stepped out of her place of divine obedience, and Queen Esther stepped into her place of divine order. Esther then accepted the challenge to become the real Queen. This story is a remarkable demonstration of a woman's divine destiny and purpose.

Esther was most recognized for her sacrifice, commitment, and determination to follow the leading of the Lord. She was fragranced with the oil of gladness and anointed by the hand of God to be in a place of providence, in the right place at the right time. Esther operated with tolerance and perfect timing, she knew when to use her tongue as she entered into the King's presence to expose the evil plan that was devised against her people. God is requiring women to be like Esther for such a time as this. *[Esther 4:14]* The book of Esther teaches us that in the time of difficulties we can find favor if we stand in our rightful place. Esther had power in her place, and because of her position in Christ, God honored her request and anointed her household. From these spiritual achievements, Esther became a lady champion.

---

*"A woman's position is to know: when to act,
when to answer, and when to move, a place of grace"*

Prayer

Father, in the name of Jesus,
Thank You for purifying my soul with Your truth.
Create in me a pure heart; renew the right spirit within me.
Lord, You created me to express my behavior in a graceful manner.
Help my behavior to honor and please You.
Teach me to find that place of grace. Place me in a position to be
blessed.
I praise You for being a God of truth.
In the matchless name of Jesus,
Amen.

Victory: A supreme triumph

Strategy 7

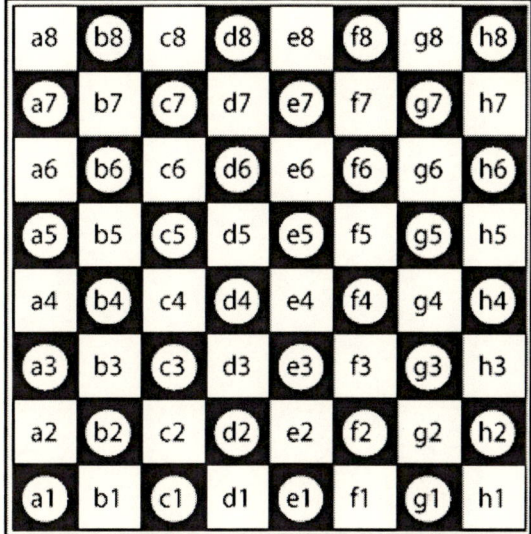

Understanding the opponent

---

*The King can move one square in any direction, horizontally,
vertically, or diagonally, to gain victory over his opponent.*

Strategy 7

Understanding the opponent

our objectives when playing chess are to take more of your opponent's pieces before they take yours, eliminating their ability to capture your King. You need to focus on how to:

a. *Capture your enemy piece first*

b. *Capture a stronger piece with a weaker piece*

c. *Capture a piece which is attacked more times than it is defended*

d. *Observe when and if your opponent is trying to take one of your pieces*

e. *Project your next move in advance to ensure that your opponent cannot successfully take any of your pieces.*

You also need to learn and remember basic chess tactics, and understand the difference between chess tactics and chess strategies. Always remember that the King is the most important piece in the game. He can also move in any direction, but he is limited to a disciplined pattern. *(See diagram 7 on page 59).*

The opponent's strategy to win in the game of chess is defined by strong defensive thinking patterns. The Queen's position in the chess game can be compared to a woman's place in the home. This position is to support and assist the King by all means necessary. As it is in the game of chess the Queen's defense moves are strategically positioned to checkmate the King's opponent, it is duly noted the same for a woman in the home.

God created the woman to be a helpmate, not to be in a state of checkmate. In every case, the opponent is regarded as the adversary, better known as the devil - Satan. It is understood that the opponent will attack; he will find ways to allure, trap and overcome his opponent. Some of the enemy's schemes and crafty tactics come by way of accusations, temptations and deceptions.

The most effective scheme is by way of deception. If the enemy can appear and pose as a refuge, allowing the spirit of deception to enter, then he has won that battle. The enemy is our opponent and we should use our defensive thinking patterns to overcome his schemes. Satan set out to defy the Word of God from the beginning, as he is determined to do also in these last days. To overcome Satan and his wicked devices we must use the weapon of the scriptures. The scripture, *2 Corinthians 10:4* says; "For the weapons of our warfare are not carnal, but mighty through God to pulling down strongholds" To successfully overcome, we must pull down those strongholds which are used as Satan's weapons against us. Many times Satan's wicked schemes and tricks are forms of deception. Scripture also speaks of how weapons would be formed against us, but they would not prosper. *[Isaiah 54:17]*

Understanding the opponent means understanding that your battle should be in the outer courts of your kingdom, not in the inner courts. Meaning, a woman's weapon against the real opponent is being in her place, and standing upon the word of God. It is in her place that she will hear a word from God. It is in her place that flesh can have no power over her. It is in her place that she will have rest.

The scripture *I Kings 19:9-15* helps us clearly understand who the opponent is and how to determine our strategy for the opposition. The enemy will send discouraging answers to spiritual questions, but if you are seeking the truth, you will find that final Word given to you by God. Elijah understood that Jezebel was a Baal worshipper and that she was directly under the influence of demonic forces. Elijah recognized the valuable lesson to identify the spirit of deception, and then walked in the strength of God's deliverance.

Remember Lot's wife? *[Luke 17:32]* Not much is said about her character, but what is said is that she looks back and becomes an unresponsive monument of bitterness (she became a petrified rock). Lot's wife did not demonstrate the spirit of obedience regarding the safety of her household. Consequently, she suffered severely for her complacency, compromise and curiosity for what was back in the city of Sodom.

The opponent seeks one to be deceived and confused as Lot's wife. She made the decision in her heart to turn back and see what was left behind instead of moving forward to see what was ahead. Lot's wife is our example of how understanding the opponent is vital to being prayerful and discerning what is the will of God.

Being a vessel of sanctification and honor can eliminate a lot of ungodly consequences that are strategically positioned to challenge God's plan for our lives. Because of God's grace and protection, we can find rest in a place of surrender to Him. In the game of chess, the Queen is in opposition, but only with the King's opponent. Therefore, as women today, we are not to find our place standing in opposition with the man; we have to remember that he is not the enemy. The Bible teaches that we fight not against flesh and blood, but that our warfare is spiritual. [Ephesians 6:12] We must remember that the man is **not** the enemy.

A man should be able to find simplicity, reassurance and tolerance in the strength of a woman.

Prayer

Father, in the name of Jesus,
I am so grateful that I have been delivered from the hands of my
enemy.
For Your Word says, there will be weapons formed against me, but
they shall not prosper.
I know that the weapons of my warfare are not carnal, but mighty
through You. I pull down all strongholds that come to destroy my
knowledge of You.
I have put on the whole armor that I may be able to stand
against the tricks of the devil,
for I know that as he comes to steal, kill and destroy, you come
that I may have life.
I declare that I am more than a conqueror, and that I am
encouraged to fight a good fight of faith as I lay hold on eternal
life.
I praise You for being a God of Peace.
In the matchless name of Jesus,
Amen.

Humble: A quiet strength

Strategy 8

Test, Evaluate,
and Improve Your Game

*When a player cannot make a legal move but is not in check,
the player is said to be stalemated. In a case of a stalemate,
the game is a draw.*

Strategy 8

Test, Evaluate, and Improve Your Game

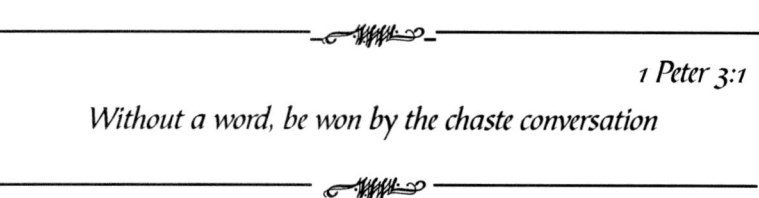

1 Peter 3:1

Without a word, be won by the chaste conversation

When a player cannot make any moves, and he is not in check, then the player is said to be stalemated. *(See illustration 8 on page 67)* It is sometimes difficult to test or measure ourselves when we are not in the will of God. We sometimes find ourselves in a position of stalemate with God. We cannot see the way to move forward and we cannot take the chance on going backwards.

It is in the flesh where we lose that connection with the spirit. Being in the right position with God improves the outcome in all our endeavors. The Queen is tested by many players and she has to make the right move to satisfy all players involved. She sets the tone for the game to be played, as well as how it will end. The Queen is crowned with glory and honor by grace; her movement and actions should follow accordingly. The Bible says that, " you may test and prove what is that good and acceptable, and perfect will of God" [Romans 12 :2] The Scripture also says to "examine ourselves to know whether we be in the faith" [2 Corinthians 13:5]. A woman has to have a plan and a purpose and must understand the consequences before she moves in any direction or makes any decisions.

To improve our game, we must understand that God always has a test of purpose, a plan for growth and the provisions of faith that will help us master his ultimate will. This is a proven way to measure our level of obedience and submission to God. For we know that we can always improve our game with more forgiveness and love. Test, evaluate and improve your spirit by the nature and spirit of Christ. Walk in grace, that you will not be overcome with evil. Test your faith that you shall know the truth. Improve your character that you may walk in the spirit of love. Evaluate your level of wisdom that you shall not be deceived. Mary, Jesus' mother, was tested, evaluated and approved by God. She was in a position of humility, submission, and faithfulness. The scripture says in [Luke 1:28] "Blessed art thou among women." Mary's place was a place of purity as a virgin who was to be married. Because of her Godly position, God chose Mary. She was honored and highly favored by God because of her position and her place as a virtuous woman. God choose her among many women because of her place of submission to him. Mary said, "Behold the handmaid of the Lord; be it unto me according to thy word." [Luke 1:38] Because of her submission, the Holy Ghost came upon her.

Another example is the woman with the issue of blood. She was also tested. In light of her faithfulness, she was made whole. For 37 years she struggled with misfortune and being misunderstood. She evaluated her situation, brought it to Jesus and improved her game by stretching out on faith and having the desire to be touched by God; it was then she was made complete in him. Many of us need to be healed and made whole in Christ before we can pursue any other challenge. Many times because of a broken heart or because we have endured much pain physically and mentally, we decided to take charge and determine what will be our results. This attitude poisons our faith and distorts our focus on God. When we are in our position and in our place, God will send his anointing to honor our prayers and bless our household. God honored Mary's prayer and delivered the woman with the issue of blood. These ladies acknowledged that they had a place and found peace in the place that God put them; these ladies had a vision of victory for their virtue!

"A woman's game improves once she understands
that God always gives a test of purpose,
a plan for growth and the provision for faith."

Obedience: To surrender thoughtfully

Prayer

Father, in the name of Jesus,
Lord, help me to commit to the submission of change.
Lead me into your good, acceptable, and perfect will.
Abide in my home and set the atmosphere of a sweet savor.
Show me how to improve, test, and evaluate my speech
in such a way that will honor you.
Heal me, O Lord. Heal my past, heal the wounds and pains
which have controlled me and my conversations.
Teach me to guard my heart with all diligence, for out of it flow
the issues of life.
Examine me, O Lord, and prove me, try my heart.
Teach me to speak your truth in love.
I declare that I am transformed by the Holy Spirit.
Thank you for being a God of change.
In the matchless name of Jesus,
Amen.

Strategy 9

Positioning Yourself

Pawns that reach the last row of the board are promoted. When a player moves a pawn to the last row of the board, he replaces the pawn by a Queen, rook, knight, or bishop (of the same color).

Strategy 9

Positioning Yourself

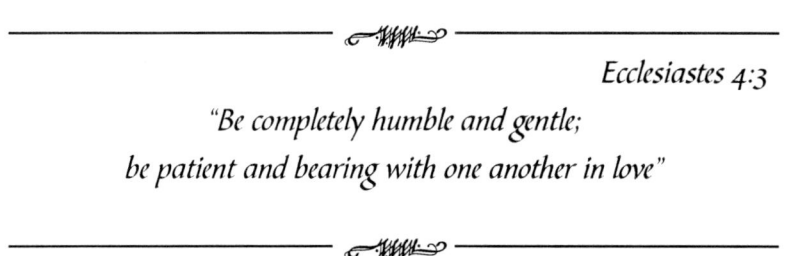

Ecclesiastes 4:3

"Be completely humble and gentle;
be patient and bearing with one another in love"

$\mathcal{T}$he pawn moves are different from the others, also when it comes to capturing the opponent they move differently. When a pawn is not capturing, it only moves one square at a time, as a straight forward move. When this pawn has not moved at all, the pawn may make a double step straight forward. When capturing, the pawn goes one square diagonally forward. *(See diagram 9 on page 75)* The player makes moves based on rules, and above all, using good judgment throughout the game. These moves hold true when a woman positions herself to move forward in Christ.

The Queen is positioned next to the King at the beginning of the game, but she can be out front, beside and or behind him at any time. It is behind him that she has preserved the power to assist him in leadership at any given time. The woman who touched the hem of Jesus' garment was positioned to be touched and healed. Her position was behind him, and that is where she was made whole. [*Matthew 9:20*] An unknown person coined an old famous cliché: "behind every good man is a good woman." This unnamed woman in the Bible displays her faith at the risk of coming out in a crowd of scorners that would possibly stone her. She pressed her way to find healing, she said in her heart, "but if I can just touch him, my life will never be the same." Her faith brought her into a place of wholeness.

As women of God, our focus should be to position our responsibilities concerning the things of God and to strongly consider our place of order. In our vast roles as housekeepers, wives, and as employees, we find ourselves spending time searching to identify our true roles as women. The key to conquering this is having a willing attitude. Your attitude should be that of Christ. In first Corinthians chapter eleven, Paul helps us understand our role by explaining that the first century church knew this, and understood that God so lovingly, wisely and sovereignly created a place for the woman and for that reason she should have an attitude suited to her God-ordained role. According to the Bible, there is a game plan for two types of women and each has her place and position. One is the married women and the second is the single women. It is important as married and single women to know and understand the difference between what is urgent, and what is a priority when it comes to their position.

Our priority as married women is to master the task of reverencing our husband, and to skillfully maintain a level of balance in our homes and on the job. Paul suggests that if you are a single woman, you are to care for the things of the Lord that you may be holy both in body and spirit. *[1 Corinthians 7:34]*

Regardless of a woman's relational status, a woman has her place in every situation. A woman in position is being placed in grace to operate in wisdom. A woman in her *position* has power in her *place,* and God will honor her request and anoint her home. Your position in Christ is relative to your spiritual insight and your relationship with Christ. Your position of surrender to him in body, mind, and your soul, should all be aligned with the will of God. A woman's position is to know her place in grace, when to act, when to answer, and when to move. Below are those two (2) positions of surrender:

1. **Married** – Your position of responsibility is to surrender to your husband. God will get the glory in your obedience to His Word. Your husband will get the honor of respect which will humble him to compromise. Total surrender to God is to compromise.

2. **Single** – Your position of responsibility is to surrender to God. He will get the glory. Your life will be a living testimony and you will be a witness of faith.

Queen Esther positioned herself to surrender by deciding "if I perish, let me perish" because she was going to see the King and do the will of God. *[Esther 4:16]* Esther put on her royal apparel, and stood in the inner court of the King's castle; she obtained favor in the sight of all that looked upon her glory. Her petition and request was granted by the King. The Bible states in *[1 Corinthians 11:7-9]* that "but the woman is the glory of a man, for the man is not of the woman, but the woman of the man."

Queen Esther was presented as a vessel of beauty to the King. During the Bible days, the King desired to show the people his

Queen's royal beauty and glory. Esther became the glory of her King, her King's personal champion. Our best move is being positioned by glory. In the game of chess, each player's side of the chessboard is determined by chance. Each player is positioned to protect their character, and then to move accordingly. A woman should position herself to make the right move for the protection of her castle versus making the first move to prove her position. Eve made the first move, and lost her position to Satan, placing mankind in a state of spiritual ruin unto this day. Patience is vital in any game of strategy; it will separate the winners from the losers.

Ladyhood
A state of womanhood that demonstrates grace
by revealing the spirit of meekness.

Prayer

Father, in the name of Jesus,
Dear Lord, position me to be completely humble.
I ask you to help me to find time to seek my role as a woman.
Help me to skillfully master the task of balancing work, friends,
home and my family.
I am a virtuous woman; I am gentle, meek, and patient in all my
affairs.
I have power in my place.
I declare that I am honored and highly favored.
Thank You for being a God of truth.
In the matchless name of Jesus,

Amen.

Strategy 10

The Art of Winning

---

*A player can resign the game, meaning that he has lost
and his opponent has won the game.*

Strategy 10

The Art of Winning

Ecclesiastes 7:8
"Better is the end of a thing than the beginning thereof;
and the patient in spirit is better than the proud spirit."

Essentially, the goal of the chess game is to make that one strategic move to capture the opponent's King. *(See diagram 10 on page 83)* Our goal in life as women is to be captured into a state of grace. The demonstration of self-control and being a pure vessel is worthy of a supreme triumph. We find ourselves captured by things of this world. Like Adam and Eve fell into temptation we find ourselves tempted as well. Our personal victory is to overcome the world. "This is the victory that has overcome the world, even our faith" [I John 5:4] Even Jesus celebrated victory when he triumphed over the temptation of Satan. He gave his promise that those who trust in his power would find victory. This promise teaches us that winning equates to victory. Conquering our temptations will be a major move to becoming spiritually victorious.

The art of winning is the art of patience, and it takes much patience to win. I agree with Dr. J. Vernon McGee, of the "Thru the Bible" radio broadcast in Pasadena, California, who stated that "endurance combined with an eagerness to win is patience." Having the patience to overcome obstacles will be our challenge to remain as Holy, sanctified and honorable women before God. This can be mastered by becoming a lady champion. We are to be careful not to find ourselves playing a mind game of trying to entrap the man in order to win him, or to use schemes or tactics to hinder him from having the freedom to be a man. Only patience can deem one victorious. By understanding your place and upholding a higher standard, the man will be challenged to stand as King and expand his authority to lead as commanded. This is why it is important to view challenges as survival strategies of life and to not focus on trying to win at any cost. There is a time in everyone's life where the challenge becomes a sacrifice. Fortunately, there is no challenge that cannot be overcome if your marching orders are given to you by God. It is perfectly human to want to win trophies or prizes without the method to conquer them. To become a winning player, one's strategy has to include a state of mastery and an attitude of grace. In the Bible, if Rebekah, Bethuel's daughter, had exhibited any pride on the day Abraham's servant appeared and requested water for himself and his camels, she would have missed God's victory for her life. [Genesis 24: 16-21] The story of Abraham seeking a bride for Isaac teaches us a lot when it comes to dating and marrying in the will of God. The servant prayed specifically for a sign, he prayed with great faith, he requested a specific sign to be established concerning who would be his wife. Rebekah completely fulfilled this sign; she gave a drink of water to the servant, and drew water for his camels. This was exactly what he asked God to do; this was his sign that Rebekah was his wife. Rebekah was God's choice to be Isaac's wife. Rebekah's attitude of grace, sacrifice, compassion, and humility made her mighty in spirit and a winner over the challenges she faced. James 4:6 teaches, "God is opposed to the proud, but gives grace to the humble." The art of winning is not only patience, but demonstrating a standard of integrity, having the desire for Godly things and possessing the attitude of grace. [Psalms 84:11] explains the value of Rebekah's grace, it states: "For the Lord God is a sun and a shield; no good thing will He withhold from those who walk uprightly." Rebekah, being in a position to be a servant ushered her in the place of a new life, a life of royalty. She was strategically positioned to win!

"The art of winning is not only patience, but demonstrating a standard of integrity; having the desire for Godly things and possessing the attitude of grace."

Prayer

Father, in the name of Jesus,
I am so grateful that I can come before Your awesome presence.
I come to You as humble as I know how. I am asking You to help
me accomplish Your purpose for my life.
Lord, help me to focus on the goal of becoming more like You.
I am a winner over life's obstacles and disappointments.
I am victorious as I move into a place of patience.
I declare that I will win by the power of faith.
I declare that the devil is defeated and, God, You are exalted in my
life.
I praise You for being a God of victory.
In the matchless name of Jesus,

Amen.

"Lady Champion:
A woman who continues to conquer every
obstacle with the spirit of wisdom.

Appendix

Recommended Reading

Briscoe, Jill. *Designing Effective Women's Ministries*, Grand Rapids, MI, Zondervan Publishing House, 1995.

Clouse, Bonnidell & Robert G. Clouse. *Women in Ministry: Four Views*, Downers Grove, IL, InterVarsity Press, 1989.

Doyle, Laura. *The Surrendered Wife: A Practical Guide to Finding Intimacy, Passion, and Peace with Your Man*, New York, NY, Fireside publishing, 1999.

Elliot, Elisabeth. *Discipline: The Glad Surrender*, Grand Rapids, MI: Fleming H. Revell, 1982.

Elliot, Elisabeth. *Faith That Does Not Falter*. New York, NY: Fireside, 2000.

Elliot, Elisabeth. *Passion and purity: Learning to Bring Your Love Life Under Christ's Control*, Grand Rapids, MI, Fleming H. Revell, 1984.

Elliot, Elisabeth. *Let Me Be A Women*, Tyndale House Publishers, 1999.

Elliot, Elisabeth. & Nancy Leigh DeMoss. *Lies Women Believe: And the Truth that Sets Them Free*, Libertyville, IL, Moody Publishers, 2002.

Elliot, Elisabeth. *What Is the Difference? : Manhood and Womanhood Defined According to the Bible*, Wheaton, IL, Crossway Books, 1990.

Hiebert, Edmond D. *An Introduction to the New Testament*, Vols. 1-3, Gabriel Publishers, 2003.

Jackson, John Paul. *Unmasking the Jezebel Spirit*, Streams Publications, North Sutton, NH, 2002.

Pierce, Ronald W. *Discovering Biblical Equality: Complementarity Without Hierarchy*, Downers Grove, IL, InterVarsity Press, 2004.

Piper, John & Wayne A. Grudem, *Recovering Biblical Manhood and Womanhood: A Response to Evangelical Feminism*, Wheaton, IL, Crossway Books, 1991.

Saucy, Robert L. *Women and Men in Ministry: A Complementary Perspective*, Chicago, IL, Moody Publishers, 2001.

Luke	1: 38	62
Luke	17: 32	56
Romans	12: 2	61
I Corinthians	7: 34	67
I Corinthians	11: 3	18
1 Corinthians	11: 7-9	67
I Corinthians	11: 8-12	13
II Corinthians	10:4	60
II Corinthians	13: 5	61
Ephesians	4: 2	66
Ephesians	5: 2	132
Ephesians	5: 22-25	20
Ephesians	6: 12	57
Philippians	2: 5-8	33
Philippians	4: 6	72
Colossians	3: 18	20, 33
1 Thessalonians	4: 4	55
1 Timothy	2: 11-13	19
I Timothy	2: 12, 13	13
2 Timothy	2: 7	17
Titus	2: 3	21
Titus	2: 5	71
Hebrews	2:1	9
James	1: 17	72
James	4: 6	40
1 Peter	3: 1-7	60
1 Peter	3: 4	44
I John	2: 16	19
I John	5: 4	39

"CheckMate" is a much needed book for the 21st century. Dr. Tyler's comparison of the critical relationship between men and women to the players on a chessboard is an insightful approach to this issue.

The use of a chess players provide an excellent analogy to the positive and negative impact that women have in the game of life. Dr. Tyler uses God's Word to expose the purpose that God had in creating women and the character needed to achieve it victoriously.

Finally, the much-debated issue of femininity is addressed with scripture and practicality. Both Christian women and men should be challenged and encouraged in their relationships after reading this book.

Debra L. Kralka
Dallas Theological Seminary

Source Notes

1. The American Heritage Dictionary of the English Language. New college ed. Boston: Houghton, 1985.

2. Stanley, Charles. "In Control." In Touch, 11 June 2003.

3. The Concise Matthew Henry, Commentary on the Bible, verse 16 of chapter 3. The Concise Matthew Henry, Commentary on the Bible, verse 18 of chapter 2.

4. 100 New Testament Sermon Outlines, John Phillips, Kregal publications. Page 93.

5. http://www.bibleone.net/print_sbs79.html, Systematic Bible Studies Genesis Chapter 3: 1-24

6. http://www.bibleone.net/ print_sbs79.html, Systematic Bible Studies, Genesis 3:1-24

7. Words to live by for women, Bethany House Publishers, 2004, Grand Rapids, Michigan. http://www.bethanyhouse.com.

8. The John Phillips Commentary Series, Exploring 1 Corinthians: An Expository Commentary, Kregal Publications. 2002.

9. The Veil, Cross TV, Word Pictures notes & outlines. Boca Raton, FL.

Strategy One
The Art of the Game
Seek uncompromising wisdom

Strategy Two
The Art of Sacrifice
Possess strength and dignity

Strategy Three
The Art of the Defense
Submitting in the fear of God

Strategy Four
Using Practical Techniques
Be self-controlled and pure

Strategy Five
Knowing when to Move
Possess a meek and quiet spirit

Strategy Six
The Portrait of a Queen
Possess the characteristic of nobility

Strategy Seven
Understanding the Opponent
Be a vessel of sanctification and honor

Strategy Eight
Test, Evaluate, and Improve Your Game
Possess chasten conversations

Strategy Nine
Positioning Yourself
Possess a humble and gentle spirit

Strategy 10
The Art of Winning
Possess a spirit of patience

BOOK YOUR NEXT EVENT WITH
Dr. Terri D. Jackson-Tyler

This dynamic speaker presents inspirational seminars and workshops for school, organizations and churches, including women's retreat and special events!

Counseling coach sessions are now available. Call for private and/or group counseling.

Dr. Terri D. Jackson-Tyler provides a proven 21- day consecration counseling program that will bring spiritual intimacy into your life.

This program is a process of dedication, sanctification and purification through consecration

Call now to start your spiritual program

For booking and more information, contact: Focused Women - 214-642-4717 ·www.focusedwomen.com· focusedwomen@mail.com· www.2checkmate.com P.O. Box 3243, Cedar Hill, TX 75106-0542

FOCUSED WOMEN

Join our monthly focus group; our discussion topics are guided to maintain higher values in our conversation, conduct and character according to scripture.

This ministry is three-fold; a discussion, support and social interaction group that offers knowledge through group communication.

Our goal is to bring unity and accountability by setting a higher standard of integrity and becoming women of wisdom without compromise.

Call the focusline to place your prayer request or just to listen to our monthly message to stay focused.
972-293-5557

Learn more about us at www.focusedwomen.com and feel free to email us at focusedwomen@mail.com

Success was failure for me. Failure became the main event in my life that brought about the greatest service to God. Being a yielded servant has brought about my greatest success.

A Place of Grace

Am I out of my place because the man is absent and
I must lead because there is no one there to follow?

Am I out of place because I have to over compensate
For the men who are present, but not willing to lead?

Am I out of place because I over work to fill the emptiness
Of loneliness, and my children suffer as a result of my selfishness?

Am I out of place because I am often aggressive
And possess a strong attitude of confidence?

Am I in this place in spite of
Or instead of?

Am I?

Where is that place of comfort?
Place of safety?
Place of gladness?
Place of security?

Can I find that place?
Can I find my inner strength?
Can I find that reflection of a strong woman?

Or should I seek to become a woman of wisdom?
Is that the secret of my strength?
Is that the place that leads me to take charge, or is that place taking
charge of me?

Where can I find that place?
Is it not true that a woman in her place is a woman in grace?

I must find that place, where I can hide,
that place where my flesh will be denied
that place where I can hear and obey
that place at His feet where I can stay.

That special, sacred, sanctified place,
is in "a place of grace."

CheckMATE

A Woman's Place
The Ultimate Challenge

To order online go to:
Authorhouse.com, www.2checkmate.com **or Barnes&Nobles.com**

Printed in the United States
219341BV00002B/22/P